THE TRUTH ABOUT MY REALITY

A Story on Escaping Abuse

ROCHELLE WRIGHT

**The Truth About My Reality
A Story on Escaping Abuse**

Copyright © 2019 by Rochelle Wright
All rights reserved.

This book or any portion thereof may not be reproduced, distributed or used in any manner whatsoever, including graphics, photography, or information storage without the express written permission of the publisher except for the use of reprints in the context of brief quotations, references, or book reviews.

Unless otherwise indicated, any scripture quotations are from the Holy Bible, King James Version. All rights reserved.

Printed in the United States of America

ISBN 978-1-733-95530-0

THE TRUTH ABOUT MY REALITY

A Story on Escaping Abuse

Dedication

This book is dedicated to my two amazing kids, you guys are my motivation, you are the reason I strive to be a better version of myself every day. To my mom, you are the strongest person I know, thank you for always loving me and motivating me to be better than you were. I've watched you struggle to make ends meet; the most important thing you could ever teach me was perseverance.

Table of Contents

Introduction

Everything that we believe to be, is not always as it should be ... ~Unknown Author

I always dreamed of having a home with bright green grass, white picket fences, rose petals blooming in a garden, and a loving household with two parents who adored me and would shower me with unconditional love.

Here I am, born and raised in one of the more rural areas in Kingston, Jamaica where there was no bright green grass, white fences and rose petals. Hell, there wasn't even the loving household with two parents. Instead, I had one parent – my mom; and we can thank my dad for that. Being raised in a single parent household, I watched my mother struggle to keep a roof over our heads, robbing Peter to pay Paul, and even then, somebody still didn't get paid. I saw a lot and endured even more, yet I was determined to make a better way out of what seemed like no way.

At age 14, I migrated to the United States - Fort Lauderdale, Florida to be exact; only to be faced with new struggles and obstacles that unbeknownst to me, would turn my world upside down and force me to have to make some very tough decisions in love, family, and life.

The Beginning

It all started in December of 1990. I was three years old ... a daddy's girl, wherever you saw him, I was not far behind... well, typically that's how it was until that one day – a day that would forever change my life.

I remember the day my father left us in Jamaica to pursue a better life in America like it was yesterday; but what I didn't know was that I would never see or speak to my father again for ten years.

The day my dad left he told me that he was coming back the next day; so, as a three-year-old would, I cheered him on as he walked on the tarmac to the airplane. I saw my mom crying and I remember telling her not to cry because daddy is coming back tomorrow; she looked at me and forced a smile and led me home. Upon arriving home that day, I anxiously waited and began thinking of all the things I wanted to do with daddy when he returns. My mom said I had a hard time sleeping because I was so anxious.

The next day, I got up at the crack of dawn anticipating daddy's return, but he never made it home. Days turned into months, months turned into years and I cried every single night for him. Every night for the next four years I sobbed in mommy's arms "I want my daddy", I would cry out, oblivious to what it was doing to her having seen me go through this.

By age seven I had completely given up and accepted the fact that my father will never return. I remember seeing my friends' dads bring them to school and I would get jealous because I was the only child in my class whose father wasn't there. When they would question where he was, without hesitance, I began telling my friends that my father was dead so that I wouldn't feel like the outcast and over time, my lie started to feel like the truth. You know what they say about a lie … when you tell the same one over and over, you start believing it to be true. Needless to say, I started believing it.

What made the lie so much more believable to me is that I don't remember my father ever calling us or writing any letters. However, mommy and I wrote him letters all the time and often, that gesture wasn't reciprocated. Although cell phones weren't popular during that time, we had access to a telephone that he could call us on if he wanted to talk to us – but he never did. Yet, we called him very often but he would never answer. This made me feel sad, unloved and forgotten by my own father. The sad part is whenever my father had something to say to us, he would call one of his friends to relay messages to us.

After my father left, my mom struggled tremendously to make ends meet. It had gotten so bad that my mother wrote a letter to my grandfather in Maryland letting him know that my father wasn't taking care of me or her and urged him to speak with my father. He would then have his friends tell mommy that he sent us $20 via western union or Money Gram and when mommy got there, there was no money. It happened so often that the last time it drove mommy to tears and she started crying in the store from embarrassment and disappointment.

During this time, my mom was working fulltime. She would leave the house around eight or nine in the morning and did not come home until about eleven at night. I remember she would get her paycheck and barely have enough to cover our rent, transportation, and utilities. We couldn't afford cable and there were times when we couldn't afford to pay for groceries in order to get a hot meal. Unlike America, Jamaica didn't have assistance available to their residents at the time, so there were no aids given, at least not that I could remember because we didn't get any; and unfortunately, if you didn't have it, you had to do without ... or simply ask for help from family or friends.

Family Intervention

Due to our struggles, my paternal grandma, my uncle on my dad's side and maternal grandparents stepped in to help us out. This was such a blessing and although at the time my uncle didn't have any kids, he treated me as if I was his daughter. My uncle would visit us several times a week and every time he visited, he had something special for us and he ended up helping mommy with most our expenses.

He was there for us so much that at one point, I remember asking mommy why my uncle can't be my daddy. That's how much of a father-figure he'd been to me. She then explained why but I was hell bent on making him my dad; after all, he did more for me than my real father ever did. Even after my uncle started having kids of his own, he never once treated me any less. Grandma helped out whenever she could as well and would also frequently visit us; and my maternal grandparents often sent us money to help with the bills and whenever we visited them in the country, they made sure we had food to take back to the city with us. While I knew mommy hated to have to lean on them for support, it was graciously appreciated and welcomed.

Conditional Parenting

As I got older, the lie I once told about my father being dead started feeling more and more like the truth. After all, it wasn't like we spoke regularly- if at all. And when we did, it so conveniently happened to be during times where I exceled or received any major accolade. I remember after taking my GSAT, I got accepted into one of the most prestigious schools in Jamaica. Word got to my father who was now living in Florida with his new wife and daughter. So, I called him and gave him the good news. That day I remember receiving praises from him, every reference of me started with "my daughter" but for me he was a little too late.

After getting accepted and realizing that the cost of tuition was way more than we've ever had, I saw my mom become so discouraged and I felt broken. We thought of different ways to come up with the money, but even that was not enough. As a result of this, at the tender age of twelve I told mommy that we should use this opportunity to get whatever we can from him.

In Jamaica, getting into high school is equivalent to getting into college here in the US; so, it is important that we excel because the competition is pretty stiff. I remember being so excited for this accomplishment but that quickly turned into terror because the tuition was $10,000. Obviously, we couldn't afford this, and we ended up getting assistance from the ministry of education where they paid some of the tuition.

That day, I called my father to tell him what school I had gotten accepted into and he ended up calling everyone he could think of to share the news. Granted, I understand that he was proud, but I really didn't like that he was telling others of my accomplishment because I felt he had no right to brag. I also noticed that he was trying to build a relationship with me after learning of my accomplishment and at that point in my life, I really didn't care to have any relationship with the man who abandoned his family.

With this newfound "relationship" I came up with an elaborate plan that would help both my mother and me. See, my mother is very honest to a fault; she wanted to tell my father everything about the assistance. I quickly told her not to and to instead tell him how much the actual tuition will be in addition to the uniform and book expenses. I wanted his ass to pay for all the heartache, hurt, disappointments and struggling we endured due to his selfishness. So, with that plan in motion, we ended up having extra money to help us out. This felt right to me … after all, he owed us years of back pay due to the struggle he caused.

First Impressions

My father and I started communicating more frequently; he even made mention of coming to Jamaica for my thirteenth birthday. I'm not going to lie, I was excited, but that excitement was not because I would meet him, I was excited for the fact that in Jamaica. It's a huge deal to have a family member from the United States visit; it's like having an A-list celebrity visit us, and that meant we would also be getting foreign items.

My father came to Jamaica on the day before my thirteenth birthday. Instead of coming to us, he had one of his friends bring me and my brother (yes, I said brother, he cheated on my mom) to the airport to see him. He had plans to take us to a resort in Montego Bay which was exciting.

When he finally got off the airplane to meet us, my excitement quickly turned into disgust. All I could think was "how could you do this to us". He walked over to my brother and gave him a hug, then hugged me and whispered in my ear "where is my kiss"? That threw me for a loop, and I remember thinking, "what the hell kind of first impression is this?" I remember responding, I don't know you like that to be kissing you. Can you believe this bastard still tried to kiss me? That's when I knew that I couldn't trust him, and I was instantly turned off by him.

We got to the resort in Montego Bay and I remember it having a huge pool. I was excited about that because I had never been in a resort pool before. I remember the outside of the hotel was all white with dark brown doors and the inside had ceramic tiles and two twin size beds. My father stated that my brother will sleep by himself and he will sleep with me. Imagine how I felt hearing this from a stranger. I had to tell him no, and when he asked, "why not", I explained to him that since he and my brother are both males its only right that they share a bed; he agreed and we went to sleep. I woke up a few hours later only to find this man in the bed with me. At this point, I opened my suitcase and made a pallet on the cold ceramic floor with my clothes, using the suitcase as my pillow.

The next morning, he acted as if nothing had happened and neither of us mentioned it. Let's be honest, what's a 13-year-old going to say to this stranger? It's my birthday and I wanted to have fun so I went with the flow of things that day.

That morning after breakfast, went to the pool and later ventured off to the beach, where we had lunch. Later that day I received a visit for my monthly friend so my fear of him trying anything with me went away. However, for the remainder of our stay he slept in the bed with me because according to him, my brother sleeps too wild for his liking.

When I got home, I told mommy everything that happened from the moment he met us at the airport to my return and she was not pleased. She was very upset ad wanted to confront him, but I convinced her not to since I had no intentions of maintaining a relationship with him.

Fear of the Unknown

After his visit to Jamaica, he would call frequently, he even allowed me to communicate with my stepmother who seemed very nice, I actually liked her more than I did him at the time because she seemed so genuine. Her an I talked almost every day and I had no doubt in my mind that when we met, our relationship would evolve.

Not long after, my father expressed that he wanted to petition for me and my brother to come the United States to live with him and his wife. My brother was ecstatic, but I on the other hand, wanted nothing to do with it. I told my mother that I didn't want to go, and she tried her best to convince me otherwise saying it's a better opportunity blah, blah, blah. I told her I did not want to leave her and she's all I had so in the end, I got my way.

That was short-lived. After a little while, I ended up having to move in with my grandma and uncle. See, my mom had a boyfriend at the time that I didn't get along with. We would get into huge arguments where we ended up yelling and screaming at each other, and unfortunately, it got physical several times. I remember the first time it happened; I was in my room watching Matlock on TV. We only had one television in the house at the time and it happened to be in my room. He came in my room wanting to watch boxing; but instead of him asking if he could change the channel, he took the remote and changed the channel. As a reaction to his rudeness, I grabbed the remote out his hand and changed the channel back to what I was watching. It was then that he walks over to the TV to change the channel back to boxing. This tug of war went on for several minutes until he got upset and hit me! He pried the remote out of my hands. I remember fighting back and, in the background, my mother kept telling me to behave myself as if I was the one in the wrong. It angered me that she took a stance in his defense. In the midst of my hurt, I told her that he was not my father and has no right to hit me or even touch my TV, and that she should never put a man before her child.

I told my uncle about the incident and he asked my mom to let me come live with him and grandma and she agreed.

Although I get my way with my mom every time, I wasn't so lucky with my grandma. I had no choice but to do everything that was required of me for my petition and my grandma made sure every appointment was kept. After it was all said and done, I was granted the opportunity to migrate to the US.

The Beginning of Hell

I entered on US soil on Sunday, July 15, 2001. I remember getting off the plane on a hot summer day in sunny South Florida, where I was met by my father and my brother. I was excited to see my brother, but very apprehensive to see my father. I greeted them both with hugs and kisses on the cheek, but that wasn't good enough for my father. He wanted me to kiss him on the lips. I immediately felt uncomfortable, as I did when we first met. I remember my father taking me sightseeing and telling me all about life in America, the schools, the culture, and he even told me about the hood (didn't know what that meant but hey, I went with it).

We got to the house where I met his pregnant wife and my three-year-old sister for the first time. All seemed well; she showed me her nice side until the very next day when my father went to work. I remember her telling me that she doesn't like boys and how much she dislikes my brother. She began to brag about all the horrible things she'd done to him since he moved in. I'm not sure why she felt compelled to share this with me. She bragged about beating him and how he is required to ask permission before he can get anything to eat! She even bragged about leaving him in Target on a rainy day because he wasn't walking fast enough for her, so he had to figure out a way home and how she makes him call her mommy. I'm floored.

As time goes by, she eventually started mistreating me too; although I never had to ask permission for food, her mistreatment came in forms of basically treating me like the black or Jamaican Cinderella. She did nothing; while my chores were to cook dinner every day, clean the house, iron my sisters' clothes, comb my sister's hair, give her a bath daily and make sure her homework is done daily. Whenever my father was around, she was a saint and as soon as he left the house, the devil will show its ugly face. The apartment we lived in didn't have a washer and dryer, so we had to go to the laundromat every Saturday. I can remember on laundry days she would wait until my father left early in the morning, and as soon as he's out the door, she would bang on the door and walls while yelling at us to wake up immediately. It was then my duty to separate all the clothes and put each pile in their respective bags and lug them to the car while she stood by and watched without any assistance. She made it perfectly clear that my brother wasn't allowed to put his clothes with ours as if his clothes were contaminated or something. As soon as we were done with bagging the clothes, she would rush us out the house before my brother and I can even get anything to eat. I clearly recall every Saturday when we got to the laundromat, she would have me and my brother do all the work while she took my sister next door to the Jamaican restaurant to get breakfast for the both of them. Sometimes they sat and ate their food at the restaurant; other times they would return to the laundromat, sit at one of the folding tables and eat their food in front of us without even offering any or asking if we were hungry. It was very clear to her that we were hungry since she didn't allow us to eat anything prior to leaving the house.

Before long, my brother and I decided that, on the night before going to the laundromat, we would pack our snacks just to have something to eat that would hold us over for the two plus hours we were washing clothes. The problem is the snacks that we had in the house were for my sister, with the exception of crackers and Capri Sun … which is what we would resort to.

I would often ask my father for money so that my brother and I could buy food to eat on laundry days.

At first, he refused; but after being asked repeatedly, he wanted to know why we needed the money. I told him and he would give me ten dollars for us to get something to eat. I believe that's when I realized just how stingy and selfish my father really was. How is it that you allow your wife to treat your children like shit? I never understood that at all.

After my youngest sister was born, things got worse; in addition to my chores, I now had the task of caring for a newborn child that I didn't birth, almost fulltime. As soon as I got home from school, my stepmother would bring my baby sister out their room and leave her in the living room for me to care for. Yes, her crib was in their room and she sleeps in there, but half the time she is in the bed with me at night. Here I am a fourteen-year-old being the mother and wife of the house when there is a well abled adult in the home; but instead she always locked herself in the bedroom - leaving both her children in the living room for me to take care of. Talk about crazy and unfair …

I remember one Saturday in October we went through our usual routine, but when we got to the laundromat, my stepmother stayed in the car with her children while me and my brother removed all the clothes and detergent from the car; we didn't even get the door closed properly before she sped off with her kids and left us standing there. My brother and I waited for her wondering where she'd gone; we had loaded all the clothes in the washing machines and the baby clothes in the dryer, but realized that she had never given us any money to start washing, so everything just sat there. An hour went by and still no sign of her. After two hours and still nothing, this gentleman walked up to us asking if he can use one of the machines since we're clearly not using it, so I let him. I figured why waste the man's time plus it was only one of the many machines we had occupied. Not even thirty minutes later, my stepmother walked in, kids in tow and of course, leftovers from what they had to eat while they were MIA. Without any explanation or care, she sat the baby down, walked over to me and asked why the clothes aren't washed. I explained to her that she left us for over two hours and didn't give us any money to wash the clothes. She then had the audacity to say why didn't you use the money your father gave you? I took a deep breath and told her that I will not use the money he gave us to wash any clothes because he gave us that money specifically to get something to eat since she refuses to feed us. *Oooh child, who told me to say that?* Stepmother grabbed me by my shirt collar and preceded to point in my face telling me what she was going to do to me and how dare I not use my measly ten dollars to wash the clothes. I kindly pried her fingers off of me one by one and told her that she has no right to grab my clothes considering she didn't buy it. Of course, she didn't let go; instead she dragged me out the door by my shirt. I overheard a young lady saying to her mom "omg this girl is arguing with her mom; I replied that she was not my mother, will never be my mother, and do not have what it takes to be my mother.

There was a telephone booth right outside the laundromat. She proceeded to slap me in the face and tried to slam my head in the wall and that's when all hell broke loose and we started fighting. I continuously punched her in the face, while she grabbed ahold of my hair. My brother attempted to pull her away. She then turned to my brother and told him to let her go and stop holding her. We were going at it for a while; then this heffa had the nerve to call me a bitch and threatened to tell my father! I laughed and told her "it takes one to know one". See, I didn't want to call her a bitch and risk her lying on me to my father because she always does, and in his eyes, we are always wrong, and she is always right. I told her go ahead and call … I don't care. On the way home, she kept spewing out idle threats and told me that I better be scared, and watch what's going to happen when she tells her mother and sister and she going to have them come to the U.S from England to beat me up. I kindly told her to let them come so I can beat both their asses too! Anyway, we got home. Her face and neck were bloodied and she gets on the phone with her mother and sister in England to give them the lowdown on what went down between me and her. As soon as my father walked through the door, she went in their bedroom and locked the door; of course, she was playing the victim as usual. About an hour later, my father walked out the room and called a family meeting, minus her of course. He asks, 'what happened between you and your step-mother today?' So my response was, "I'm sure she already told you but here's my side." I started telling him how she had us taking everything out the car by ourselves, sped off before we could get the door closed properly and had us waiting over two hours for her to return and in the middle of me explaining myself, he cuts me off by calling me a liar and saying she would never do anything like that (I think that's one of the only times my father didn't call me a bitch, whore and a slut while scolding me). He looks over to my brother and asks if that was true and he said yes, and he proceeds to yell at him too.

The next day me and my brother waited for the church bus to come get us like we do every Sunday. Got to church and was blindsided by all the questions the elders had for me as a result of yesterday's activities. See, unbeknownst to me, my stepmother and my father called every single church member I had a close relationship with and told them that I attacked her and beat her up without any back story portraying me as the aggressor. So here I am, having to explain myself to a bunch of people who had no knowledge of the hell I was living in.

Later that night, my father, brother and I went back to church for the six o'clock service, and when it was done, my father decided that instead of going straight home, he would make a detour and go to a church members home who I was extremely close with to discuss what happened between me and his wife. So, we're at her house in her daughters' room while this lady and my father are in another room having a lengthy conversation about me. After a while, the church sister came in the room, removed her daughter, and began asking questions about the altercation. I was very candid with her and told her everything that had transpired. I told her about how my step-mother had us doing everything around the house without lifting a finger, how she pretty much almost ran me and my brother over with the car, how she disappeared for over 2 hours leaving us at the laundromat without food, the fight and her calling me a bitch. She was very empathetic and told me that my stepmother was wrong and asked if it was ok for her to discuss the information I shared with my father and I told her that I really didn't care, it's not like he'll believe me.

A little after midnight he finally decides to leave. We got to the car, my brother sat in the back while I sat in the front, our father got in the car slammed the door then yells "Rochelle how the hell you going to lie and say that your step-mother called you a bitch!?" I responded with sleep filled eyes 'she did call me a bitch'. His response, yelling of course, was 'stop telling lies; she would never say anything like that'. My response, 'it's true! You can ask my brother'. He turns to look at my brother in the backseat, 'and asks is that true? Did your step-mother call Rochelle a bitch?' My brother confirmed that she did and my dad yelled back at him 'stop telling lies; you're only saying that because you don't like her.' My brother responded that he was not lying and my father told him to shut up. We drove home in silence.

The next day, I wake up, got ready for school, and try to wake my father up so that he can take me to the bus stop, and he doesn't answer me. Instead, he purposely gets himself ready late so that I can miss the school bus, which meant that I would have this long, awkward ass drive to North Lauderdale. We drove in silence the entire time and as we come to a stop at the light adjacent to the school, I exit the car and slammed the door. He rolls down the window asking if I'm going to say goodbye. I barely open my mouth and say bye!

I remember a few weeks prior to the fight, my father sat me down in the living room and told me that he wanted me to call my stepmother "mommy". I looked at him in disbelief and tell him that I will never call her that because after all, she is not my mother. His response was that while I was living there, she was my mother. I replied 'no she's not, she's my stepmother and there's a huge difference; plus I didn't come out of her vagina so the answer is no.' I said, I will be calling her by her name.

She didn't like the fact that I refused to call her mommy and to make matters worse, my brother stopped calling her mommy as well, so that too, fueled her hatred towards us. When my father was around, she was such a saint and caring parent towards my brother and me, but as soon as my father left the house, the devil resurfaced. What's even more frustrating was the fact that me and my brother couldn't talk to our father about anything, especially when it comes to his precious wife.

In high school, I dreamed of one day attending a prestigious university, so I applied myself with hopes of achieving that goal. I remember giddily telling my father that I wanted to attend either Georgia State or University of Miami, only for him to respond saying "why you even talking about going to college? You will never be anything in life, you're not going to college and I am not paying for you to go to any college, so you better get a full scholarship."

The entire four years I've been in high school, I've been on the honor roll almost every semester. I remember bringing home the honor roll breakfast invitation and handing it to my father only for him to throw the invitation on the floor and say "what the hell is this? I'm not going to that foolishness." Being that I was the only student who didn't have a parent at the award ceremonies showing support, my music director at our church decided that he would come to every award ceremony after I gave him the invitation. He asked would my father or step mother be going and I told him no, explaining the situation to him.

After my father got word that the music director would go to all my honor roll ceremonies, he got mad and told me that he is not allowed to go to any more of them. This broke my heart, I felt so sad because the next ceremony was the biggest and most important one and I had no one. After the ceremony, the music director called to see how it went, and after I told him, he said that he was proud of me and I immediately broke down crying. He asked my why was I crying and I painfully told him 'because my father has never told me that he is proud of me".

I can also recall times when report cards were sent home and if I got anything less than an A plus, my father would start calling me names and telling me that I'm a dumb bitch who will never amount to anything. I would then get punished for the less than desirable grades. This went on for years. The first few times I felt very hurt, disrespected and defeated, but overtime, I had gotten so used to the abuse it really didn't bother me anymore.

See, my father is the type of person who believed that all he needed to do is put a roof over our heads and that would be sufficient. So we didn't get allowances, hell, he barley wanted to give me money to buy lunch at school so I would tell him that I didn't like the lunch that was were provided so that he can give me money, and whenever I got my weekly twenty dollars I would save it so that I can buy clothes and shoes for myself. My father and his wife didn't really buy me much clothes or shoes, and whenever they did, they made sure that they were oversized/outdated clothing, I wasn't allowed to wear heals more than an inch high, they did this all because my father didn't want another man looking at me sexually.

Every day while in that house, my father would always ask for me to give him a kiss. One night, when I first moved here, my father backed me up in the corner of our living room and told me that I need to let him bathe me sometimes. I automatically became sick to my stomach. I looked at him in total shock then said, "No!

why would I do that?" His response was "well you would let your mother bathe you, so you need to let me bathe you too." I said, "yes of course I would let her bathe me; we have the same body parts."

After that, he then told me that I needed to take a shower with him sometime. This was a gesture went on for several weeks, then escalated to him asking me for a kiss every time we encountered each other which is very often considering we live in the same house. I did notice however, that my father and stepmother would kiss on the cheek; every time he asked for a kiss, I would plant one on his cheek, but then he would make me kiss him on the lips.

He Touched Me

One night, my siblings and I were getting ready for bed as usual and my father came in our room and suggested that we all sleep in his room with him and his wife. At first, I was reluctant; but then decided to do it because I shared a room with my brother and I wanted him to have his space, even for just one night. That night, I remember bringing my blanket in their room and making a pallet on the floor for me and my sisters. I slept with my infant baby sister in the middle and my 3-year-old sister on the end. At some point that night, I remember waking up and laying on my left side, and my father was lying behind me with hands under my shirt fondling my naked breasts. At first, I froze from the shock of it all. I was afraid to move but knew I had to so I tried to get up and he asked me where I was going. I told him that I needed to use the bathroom and it was at that moment, I locked myself in the bathroom and cried my eyes out.

Since I was a heavy sleeper at the time, I'm not sure how long he'd been violating me or if he had put his hands down my panties. All I know is that was the day any sense of security or safeness I had went out the window. I remember feeling guilty and ashamed, thinking what I could've done or said to make him feel like it was ok to molest your own child. Was it because I wore skimpy clothing at times; was it because I did not wear any bra when I went to sleep at night; was I too friendly or too inviting? I wasn't sure …

After that encounter, things seem to have gotten worse. The groping became a daily occurrence. I remember one night, my father was walking towards his bedroom while I was walking from my room, and as we walked past each other, he stopped me and asked, "where is my kiss?" I tried to give him a kiss on the cheek and he refused stating that I need to kiss him on the lips. Reluctantly, I turned around, but this time, instead of barely puckering up then wiping off my mouth, something inside me told me to fold my lips and as soon as I did, he tried to force his tongue in my mouth. I immediately back away wiping my mouth while he laughed at me. I ran into the bathroom and cried while washing my face and mouth with soap and water. The level of disgust that I was feeling was overwhelming that all I could do was cry.

I remember one Saturday afternoon, he sat me down on the sofa stating that he needed to speak to me. I sat adjacent to him but he insisted that I sit closer to him. So, I moved to the other end of the couch. He looked at me and said "you need to let me feel how big your breast is. I looked at him in shock and asked why would I do that? He responded by saying "because I'm your father and I need to know how big your breasts are." He also went on to say, "you need to let me feel how big your ass is and how phat your pum pum is." As he said these things to me, I sat there thinking how disgusting and sad of an individual this man is to even think that it is ok to look at your own daughter like that.

Every time I walk by him, he would grab my breast, butt or vagina and try to kiss me on the lips. This happened so often that each encounter became a blocking match, and I'm always on the defense. The sad part about it is that his wife sees him doing this and does or says nothing about it. She would often laugh whenever he touched me as if this was a laughing matter.

Isolation

While I was living with my father, he made sure to keep me away from any and everyone who he believed could help me. I remember shortly after moving to Florida, my father forbade me from speaking with my mother who was living in Jamaica at the time. Whenever I called her, I would get in trouble and whenever she called me, he either didn't allow me to speak to her or him and his wife would pick up the other receiver and listen in on the conversation.

The church we went to was riddled with family members on my mothers' side and people who were close friends with my maternal grandparents. However, my father made sure that I didn't formally know any of them and if I knew who they were, I didn't get close to them. I was never allowed to go anywhere except for school and church three days a week and twice, sometimes three times on Sundays.

I was never allowed to talk to boys or have male friends that called the house, let alone date all because he wanted me to himself. I had to be sneaky with my male friends, I would only call them when he and his wife weren't home, and I would only see my boyfriend before I got home after school and use the same method to call him. Most times I was able to get away with talking to and seeing my boyfriend because we went to the same church.

I remember when I was in the ninth grade, there was an older gentleman stalking me. Every day while I walked home from school, he would drive by as I walked past his house and wait for me across the street from my home. By the time I noticed, I told my father who responded by telling me to stop telling lies for attention. It was in the moment that I realized that he did not have my best interest at heart. This revelation had me riddled with fear. I was afraid to walk home from school and would often pretend like someone was home by knocking on the door and talking to a fake person by asking them to open the door for me. I remember telling my then 12-year-old brother about my stalker and in his attempt to protect me, he would rush home before me and wait for me to get home so that I wouldn't be alone. But even that wasn't enough. I would often have my friends with cars or my boyfriend at the time take me home in the evenings.

I remember this one Sunday evening, I was on my way to church with a close church sister and her family and when I mentioned the stalking situation, the immediate reaction that I received from both of them saddened me and warmed my heart at the same time; they were more concerned about me and my well-being than my own father was. When they asked had I told my father I told them yes I had; however, his reaction wasn't favorable to me. They seemed concerned at how he handled the situation and to ease my mind and fear, they told their son and a friend of mine at the time to accompany me home safely.

He Hit Me

One Wednesday night in my junior year of high school my father hit me for the very first time.

A few years prior, my father started his own mobile mechanic business and quit his job after a child support situation with one of my brother's mother. Upon starting this business, my father expressed to us that this will be a family business and all of us would have to play a vital role in its success. My brother and I had no interest in the business, but we had no choice. I was made the secretary, and would earn twenty dollars per week (which I never got by the way) and my responsibility would be to ensure that all payments are collected, invoices are logged accurately, and I would also keep a log of clients with outstanding balances. Well, one Wednesday afternoon after him and his wife returned from visiting the house that was being built in Lehigh, things got a little heated. I remember being in bed sleeping after a long day at school and choir rehearsals, when he forcefully woke me up and escorted me over to his makeshift office. His wife was sitting at the dining room table adjacent to the tan chair with a smirk on her face and my father standing over me. There was an invoice I was working on two days prior; I couldn't get confirmation that the client had paid so I put the invoice in the pending file. Unbeknownst to me, his dear wife deliberately hid the check so that it couldn't be located and upon their return, she took that same invoice and placed it in her folder. My father proceeded to ask me where the hell was the invoice for the client? I sleepily told him where it was, and his response was that it was not there. I again told him where I put it and why it was there, and he began yelling at me - calling me a lying bitch. He asked repeatedly where the invoice was, and I repeatedly gave him the same response. I could see his wife laughing out the corner of my eye. And that's when my father towered over me and told me that I was a waste of time and he should've never had me or brought me to the U.S. I simply replied "okay", and that's when he started punching me in the face, head, chest and stomach. I landed on the floor and he bent over me and kept punching me in the head and stomach. All I could do was lay there crying as I was being brutally abused by my father and as his wife sat there smirking and laughing. When he was finished, I went into the bathroom and cried for about fifteen minutes more. It was that night that I decided that I was going to kill my father.

I angrily thought of how I could kill him since he always sleeps with his bedroom door unlocked. After I got out the bathroom, I tried lying down in an attempt to fall asleep, but I couldn't; every time I would lay my head on the pillow, I would feel some fluid draining inside my head. I was afraid to fall asleep because I thought I would die if I did.

As I sat up in the bed waiting for him and his wife to retreat to their room, I quietly sobbed because I didn't want to wake up my brother or have him know what had happened. Once they were in their room, I pretended to go in the bathroom and tiptoed in the kitchen and grabbed one of the silver knives. I then entered the bathroom to wipe the snot that was running down my nose, flushed the toilet then carefully placed the knife under my pillow, sat up in the bed with the pillow behind my back and waited for them to fall asleep. At some point in the night, I got up and tried to open their door, but it was locked. There, a disappointed seventeen-year-old me, went back to the kitchen and put the knife back.

The next morning, I woke up and got ready for school, as usual, I knocked on my father's bedroom door to let him know that I was ready for him to take me to the bus stop, and in his true fashion, he purposely made me miss the bus so that I would be stuck with him in a 30 minute car ride to school. The entire ride was in silence, and as we pulled up to the light adjacent to my school, I saw my best friend at the time waiting for me at the front entrance. I got out the car, slammed the door and walked off, he rolled down his window and asked if I was going to say goodbye; I yelled, "later" and kept walking.

When I got to my friend, we greeted each other but she immediately knew something was wrong. The look of concern on her face and the sheer embarrassment I felt knowing I would have to tell her was piercing my soul.

She looked at me and said "sister, your face is swollen are you ok?" and I broke down crying. She suggested we go to the nurse's office as I told her what happened. On our walk there she reassured me that everything will be alright, and she would let our first period teacher know that I wasn't feeling well and had to see the nurse.

As soon as I opened the door to the nurse's office, I saw the school resource officer and I greeted him, but because he knew who I was and saw that I wasn't my regular self, he asked if I was ok. I immediately started crying and yelling "I'm going to kill him; I don't want to live with him anymore." I told him everything that happened, and he advised me to stay in the office. He then told me that he would have to report what I told him, and I told him that I didn't care. After a couple hours, I was released to class because I had an English honors test that I needed to take. While I was taking the test, I kept dozing off and experiencing abdominal pains. My best friend noticed and told the teacher that I wasn't feeling well and needed to see the nurse. I went back in the nurse's office with excruciating pain and I could barely keep my eyes open. The nurse was concerned that I had suffered a concussion and that my appendix may have ruptured which would possibly be the cause of the pain. She told me that she will be calling the ambulance and would have to make my parents aware. I asked her not to, but by law, she had to do so anyway. My stepmother came to the school as I was escorted to Broward General Hospital.

When we got to the hospital, my fathers' wife was clearly upset. She tried scolding me about bringing in outsiders in our family situation and said I better not let anything happen to my father or I'd regret it. The doctors came in and stated that there was no concussion, but it appears that there was fluid in my abdomen, and it needed to be drained as soon as possible. I was discharged after my step-mother told the doctor that she would take me to the pediatrician for a follow up.

I remember on the ride home, she yelled and screamed at me. I remembered her saying "watch and see what your father is going to do to you when you get home". I honestly at that point didn't care anymore; so, I just sat there in silence as she kept running her mouth. We got home and my brother and father were both in the house. My brother asked was I okay and my father sent him to his room. I remember my father looking at me with disgust, but he never spoke.

After the incident, I believe the police questioned my father and stepmother because she gathered my brother and sisters in the living room and told them that if anyone asks if my father had ever hit them, they need to say no. She looked at my brother and told him he better not tell anyone anything or else they will send him back to Jamaica. She then asked my now five-year-old sister if my father has ever beaten her and she said yes; then I watched as she coerced my sister into saying no he's never laid a finger on her.

To add insult to injury, my father and step mother told the church and all their friends that I called the police on my father and lied about him hitting me. They especially told all the adults who took to me and looked at me like a daughter about this alleged lie. Days, weeks, and months went by with my father not speaking to me, and whenever I'd initiate any conversation, he would ignore me.

In June of 2004, we moved from Fort Lauderdale to Lehigh Acres. This was a huge adjustment for me. I was looking forward to entering my senior year of high school with my friends, but not only that, the love and support that I've been blessed to receive from my church family was no longer in arms reach. Needless to say, I no longer had an outlet and that made me sad. So here I am, in a new environment, no friends or family and the only person who I know for sure that I can trust is my younger brother. We were all we had.

Shortly after moving, a friend of the family came from Jamaica to spend some time with us. She was one of the few people I could talk to about what I was feeling. Of course, my father told her his version of the incident and in true fashion of his, he lied and blamed it all on me and told her that I had called the police on him. I remember her asking me about the incident and after I gave her my side, she played the role of mediator so that my father and me would get back on speaking terms.

I can remember my first day a Lehigh Senior High like it was yesterday. I felt like a fish out of water. I went from attending a charter school with a total population of roughly 750 students, to a school where my senior class alone was almost half that. Making friends didn't come easy because the demographic was different and I was this shy, seventeen year-old who didn't speak much. At my old school, there was so much diversity that it was impossible for anyone to feel left out. Each nationality had their own people there to where they would form somewhat of a clique; however, the entire student body was like one big happy family. This new school was the total opposite of what I was used to, not to mention, with everything that I was going through, I was very much an introvert.

Being in this new house brought out a more aggressive side of my father. Since I was almost eighteen, I didn't feel the need to be sneaky when it came to dating or having male friends. I remember telling my father for the first time that a boy at my school liked me, and his first and only response was "no man will ever love you the way I do, and all men want to do is get in your panties". When he said that I felt disturbed because I knew what that statement meant. The verbal abuse continued, and so did the inappropriate gestures. I was groped every day and was forced to kiss him on the lips whenever a kiss is requested and if I did otherwise, he wouldn't stop until I gave him what he want and he would try to stick his tongue in my mouth.

Throughout all this turmoil, I still managed to keep my good grades, but now that I was a high school senior, the pressure was on when it came to college applications. My school was very proactive when it came to assist the seniors with the transition, so when my guidance counselor realized that I hadn't applied to any colleges I was summoned to her office. She asked me what my plans were for college and since I was a straight A student she was concerned. I told her that my father refused to give me any money for the college applications or help me in any way possible.

I remember my guidance counselor giving me the money out her own pocket to apply to the University of Miami. She then did some research and found that Edison Community College was offering a full scholarship to some students and urged me to write my essay and I was selected. I told my father about the scholarship, but he wasn't very supportive. He told me that I'm wasting my time with this college thing because I'm a dumb bitch who will never be anything in life. I didn't let that discourage me though because as far as I knew, I didn't need him anymore and that was my way out. That was short lived through because once I had to fill out the FASFA form another obstacle presented itself. My father refused to fill out or provide any of his financial information and that was a requirement. I made the guidance counselor aware of this and she reached out to him and stated the importance of having this information. I was then told by my counselor that because he refused to provide the necessary information, my scholarship will be in jeopardy and I would not be able to attend college.

I'm not sure what happened, but my stepmother suddenly took an interest into this journey of my life and she too tried to convince my father that he needed to fill this form out, but he still refused. Much to my surprise, she went behind his back and completed the FAFSA form with all his information so that I was able to attend college in the fall. I was grateful and had now develop a newfound respect for her in that regard.

June 4, 2005

This is where things got interesting. Having witnessed for the first time the domestic abuse between my father and his wife.

This night, my brother and I stayed up late to watch TV like we always do every weekend. Around 1:30 in the morning, we decided to call it a night and go to bed. It couldn't have been no more than 30 minutes after we went to bed that my brother came and got me from all the commotion happening on the other side of the house in their room.

We tiptoed all the way over to their door and listened to them arguing. I could hear her screams while he was cursing and hitting her. As they got closer to their bedroom door, my brother and I scurried back to our rooms and pretended like we were sleeping. I remember cracking my bedroom door just a little bit so that I could see what was going on in the kitchen. I saw her pick up the blue corded phone and dial 911. And as she screamed for help, my father used the meat cleaver and chopped the phone cord disconnecting the call.

He then punched her in the face and picked up a skillet and began hitting her in the chest with it all while calling her a dirty bitch. She screamed "you bloody bastard" and ran into my room screaming for me to help. I remember locking her in my bedroom while I went into the dining room to grab a chair from the table in order to block my father from getting in. I also remember at one point trying to break them up as he was hitting her and that was the point where he grabbed my left arm and began twisting it as if he had intended on breaking it. To this day I still have the scar on my arm.

By the time the officers got to our house, my father had already left for Fort Lauderdale to be with his mistress and her kids. I called him to find out what was wrong with him based on his actions for that night and his response was "she needs to listen when big man is talking to her." I told him that was not right to put his hands on a woman and asked was he okay with his actions and he hung up on me.

The officers took statements from my father's wife and myself. My brother refused to speak on the events. After that night, a restraining order was taken out on my father and we pretty much never saw or heard him again. I remember one day we were all in the house and my father showed up out the blue and started arguing with his wife. At that point, she triggered the police alarm and they arrived within minutes, but by that time, he was gone again.

After about a week of the incident, I remember her telling me how she did not want my brother in the house. I expressed to her that he would have to stay there because he had nowhere else to go. Her response was "well your father is not taking care of us or doing anything for the kids and I can't afford to take care of him." It had to have been maybe a couple days later that she put my brother out the house.

After my brother left, things were a little intense, she ended having to get a job and I started working at the local mall to offset any additional expense. I also assumed the responsibility of taking care of the household and my sisters while mt stepmother went to work, this system was working well for the both of us; or so I though…

I essentially knew my time was coming … I just didn't know when. I remember one day I woke up to go to college and she came into my room and told me that I needed to get out because her brother told her that since I am not her child, she should not have me staying there. Naturally, I told her that I wasn't leaving. She then called the cops on me and told them that she wanted me to be out of the house immediately or else she will remove me herself. I remember the officer asking her some questions such as is this your child, and she responded, "no, this is my husband's daughter and we're not together and she cannot stay here." He then asked her how long I'd been living there and if her and my father were married and living together when I was partitioned to come in live in America. Her response was yes and that's when the officer told her that by law, although she is not my mother, her being married who my father when the paperwork was filed and when I entered America, she is legally responsible for me for 5 years and that putting me out the house is against the law. She stated her understanding and then the officers left. In that moment I felt hurt and betrayed and used, especially since in the time that my father left her, I was the one helping her around the house with the kids and with a few of the bills. I called my then boyfriend's mom who was already privy to everything that had been going on and told her about these events while she was on her way to pick me up to take me to school. I remember sitting in the back of the class crying my eyes out because I was terrified of what was to come. That same afternoon I got back to the house with my boyfriend's mother and aunt and to my surprise, there was a black trash bag sitting in the corner of the front door with all my belongings in them and the locks were changed.

That was the day I moved in with my then boyfriend, his mom and brothers. Although not the most ideal situation for an eighteen-year-old, that was the only option I had. This was the first time I experienced depression unbeknownst to me. I remember I would wake up and fall asleep crying every day, I wouldn't and the things I once enjoyed, no longer mattered, not even school. I couldn't stay focused in school because all I did was cry while I was in my classes. I wouldn't eat and I had a hard time falling asleep at night. I remember my boyfriend's mom having to go to the store to buy Ensure protein drinks so that I could supplement that for food since I wasn't eating and had lost a significant amount of weight.

I eventually saw my grades declining and even came close to losing my scholarship. I was able to stay focused enough to get a passing grade and after my first semester, I dropped out of college. At that point in time I felt so defeated, lost, unworthy and unloved; I felt like a failure. I clearly remember trying to commit suicide on several occasions, the suicidal thoughts were never ending; all I wanted was for this nightmare to end.

So here I am, a depressed eighteen-year-old college dropout, working at Macy's, with credit card debt out the ass and bouncing from couch to couch because at this point, I had also broken up with my boyfriend and had to move out. I met a dear friend who was kind enough to let me stay with her and her roommate rent free until I was able to get on my feet. I didn't have enough money to take the bus every day to work and my friend had a fulltime job, so finding transportation was my responsibility. Thankfully, I had a few friends who would take turns picking me up and dropping me off.

A New Beginning

The following September I moved to Largo, Maryland. I was living with my godmother in her mother's house. I realized that a different location didn't take away the feeling of emptiness that I had within me.

A few months before moving, I started suffering from migraine headaches. I remember the first few months of me being here, I couldn't leave the bedroom because the pain was so severe that it paralyzed me. I was only able to get up out of bed to use the bathroom; and even that was a struggle because of the severe nausea and vomiting. Over time I started feel a little better as the frequency of the migraine headaches subsided. I eventually started feeling somewhat like myself again. My godmother took me to different schools so that I could register and continue my studies. But that had its problem as well because the college I wanted to attend would not take my transfer credits; I had a feeling of defeat once again. One day, my godmother came in my room with the Washington Post and in it, she circled different schools that offered Medical Assisting programs that she thought might interest me. We decided on Sanz College and moved forward with the registration process, but I was once again faced with the issue if having my father complete the FAFSA form. Me and my father had not spoken in over a year so there was no way I was getting any information form him, we reached out to one of the financial advisors who suggesting that I used my mother's information instead; but there was one big problem, she lived in Jamaica. The financial advisor did some research and I could use my mother's information, but she needed to provide a notarized letter, property tax information, bills and a bank statement. Thankfully the information provided, and I was able to continue my studies; seven months later I graduated with a certificate as a Certified Medical Assistant.

A year later I got pregnant with my first child and was over-the-moon excited. I met my oldest son's dad in downtown Washington, DC one night as I walked to the McPherson Square train station to head home from work, we exchanged numbers and things took off from there.

During the pregnancy, made a vow to never treat my son and future kids the way my father treated my brother and me. When I gave birth, I promised my son that I would show him nothing short of love and affection and would lead by example and not with a do as I say, not as I do approach like I had been subjected to. I vowed that I would protect him at all costs, and no matter who a person is to us, I would never let anyone mistreat him.

By this time, I had broken things off with my son's father and had also gone a whole four years without speaking to my father and I was okay with that. In May of 2009, I remember visiting my uncle and his family in Fort Lauderdale. One of my aunts was coming back to the states from visiting relatives in Jamaica and my father was picking her up from the airport; and because she had brought back some goodies for me, my father had to bring her by my uncle's house. I remember when he got there, I wouldn't speak to him even after several attempts from my aunt. Unbeknownst to me, he had brought my little sisters with him. I hung out with them for a while and when it was time for them to leave, they begged and pleaded for me to come back to Lehigh Acres with them. Initially, I was very uncomfortable with the idea of me and my son being around this man, but for the sake of my sisters, I decided to go. I sat in the car for the long, uncomfortable two-hour ride. We got back to my father's house and when it was time for bed, he suggested that my son sleep with him in his room. I was immediately riddled with fear, fear that he might molest my son the way he did me. I told my older sister that I need her to keep an eye on my son and she is to sleep with him. That night, I slept uncomfortably in my sister's twin bed while my son and sisters slept together.

When I got back to Maryland, the relationship between me and my father changed. I also reenrolled in school for nursing and that was going well. We were speaking to each other again and was even trying to build a father-daughter relationship. Things were going great; we were almost like best friends. I spoke to him every day and told him everything; he would call me and do the same. Whenever he had a thought or a plan for something, he would call me first to get my opinion and vice versa, but that didn't last very long. I remember one day I was on the phone with my father talking about school and he had the nerve to tell me that he was proud of me; I couldn't remember the last time I laughed so hard. He asked why was I laughing and I told him it was a little too late for that.

About a year later, I started dating someone. I told my father about it initially and he seemed fine. The relationship between him and I was still consistent, but as soon as he realized that the relationship between me and the young man I was dating at the time were more serious than I led on, his ways started to change. He went from being a supportive father/friend, to acting like a possessive boyfriend. So, here we are again, several years later feeling like my father only sees me as a sexual being. I remember my father making snide comments about my relationship saying that the guy will never love me the way that he does, and if I go a day or even a half day without calling or texting him, he got jealous and would start asking why I haven't called or texted him. He would then say things like "it must be because of that man." It had gotten to the point where it was so unbearable, and I had to cut him off again. I felt so hurt and blamed myself because I allowed this man to enter my life and hurt me again. While I didn't have a choice as a child, I damn sure had one now that I was grown; yet, I still allowed him to make me feel the way he did all those years I was under his roof.

During that break from my father, I took the time to heal. I ended things with the guy I was seeing and decided to put my sole focus on me and my son. Life was great, we were like the dynamic duo. I fell in love with myself again. I was celibate; and most importantly, I got to know me and was able to move past all the hurt and pain. During that time, I also started dating again, this time, it was with a familiar face… a longtime friend I met right after I had my first child. Not long after things between him and I became serious and several months later I was pregnant with my second son.

In October of 2012, I went to Fort Lauderdale for one of my friend's wedding. After that I drove to Lehigh Acres to see my grandmother who lived with my father. This meant that I would also have to speak to him. He had since moved, plus I wouldn't go to his house and not speak, especially since I had company. I remember meeting up with my father at the local flea market so that he could show me where he lived. I introduced him to my boyfriend and of course, he got to see his grandson again.

When we got to his house, he decided that he wanted to get to know my boyfriend which was fine by me. What I didn't know was that he would start acting the way he did when I dated the last guy a few years back. All seemed fine at first, however, when he was done talking to my boyfriend, he asked to talk to me in his bedroom. He was asking me all sorts of questions about how we met and how long we've known each other. Questions about trust even came into play and whether I loved him. When that was over, he asked to speak with both of us together and that's when things got interesting. My father started giving us unsolicited advice. I remember him asking us what were our plans for each other and him asking my boyfriend what his intentions were. He then started asking my boyfriend about his family and wanted my boyfriend to give him his father's full name and phone number and address, I was happy that my boyfriend refused to do so. My father then looked at us and told me that my boyfriend should be my sole priority and that I should put him before my son. Both my boyfriend and I quickly shut that down and let him know that no one comes before my child, period! I also remember my father grabbing our hands and began to pray over us, but the prayer wasn't what you'd expect. This man was praying for abuse and infidelity in my relationship; I immediately got up and walked out.

Shortly afterwards, we left and drove back to our hotel in Fort Lauderdale. When we got back to Maryland, I didn't call or speak to my father; his calls and text messages went unanswered. I remember the following January, he called me one night and I finally answered. He sounded sad and defeated but I wasn't going to give in and pretend that I was okay with him or his ways. I remember the conversation started very generic with him talking about everything under the sun, then he asked, what did I do to you for you to treat me like this? I'm not going to lie, I was shocked because I never thought the day would come where my father was man enough to admit his wrong doings, accept the truth and move on.

Well, to my surprise he wasn't referring to the years of abuse. He wanted to know why I thought it was okay to tell him that I loved my boyfriend back when we visited him and my grandmother in October. Again, I was disappointed but unlike the other times, I was now on defense. I remember him distinctly asking me "how come you don't have a problem saying you love that guy, but you never tell me you loved me?" I paused, rolled my eyes, took a deep breath and told him that my mother had always told me to never say anything I don't mean. I could tell he didn't like my response, but I really didn't care. I had made up my mind then and there that he would have to address the elephant in the room. His response was, why would you tell me you love him? I immediately got upset and began to lay it all out. I said to him, what you mean why would I tell you that? You asked me if I loved him and I answered, what you want me to lie? I'm not doing that; You want to know so bad why I treat you the way I do? Have you ever stopped to look in the mirror? Look at all the things you did to me, the way you treated me." And before I could go any further, he rushed off the phone saying he had to go and hung up on me. We have not spoken since, and I'm ok with that. It is impossible to have a relationship with my father and I refuse to continuously put myself in a situation with him where he constantly makes me feel like he's my man and I'm having an affair with someone else. At this point in my life, I do not need to nor do I require a relationship with him. I honestly don't need that kind of stress in my life and he stays where he his while I live my life with my kids.

My second pregnancy was a rough one and I ended up having to once again withdraw from my studies. Life was otherwise going great, after having my son, I resumed college but not long after dropped out because of the stress of having to care for my family, go to school fulltime and work a fulltime job plus I no longer saw a future for myself in nursing. I immediately enrolled in a different University where I was able to take classes online and changed my major to Business Administration.

During this time, I was able to focus on my family and work fulltime while taking classes in the comfort of my own home. I maintained a high GPA and was an honor student throughout.

In June of 2016, I received my Associates degree and in June of 2018, I received my Bachelors' degree in Business Administration. Throughout all of life's challenges and obstacles, my faith never wavered. I sought counseling and I am still on the path to healing.

About the Author

Rochelle Wright currently resides in Maryland with her 3 children. She is sister and great friend to those close to her. She has a passion for helping others, she enjoys reading, cooking and spending time with her kids. With a shaky family background, Rochelle prides herself on being the rock for her siblings and the anchor for her immediate family.

Rochelle currently works in corporate America as a Human Resources professional.

www.ingramcontent.com/pod-product-compliance
Lightning Source LLC
Chambersburg PA
CBHW030825060726
47590CB00004B/1400